XIOMARA.b

WE HAVE MANY SIDES, WHAT'S YOURS?

A SERIES OF POEMS THAT CONNECTS MILLENNIALS IN A WORLD OF CHAOS.

ISBN-13: 978-1-63616-031-3

Published by Opportune Independent Publishing Company

For permission requests, write to the publisher, addressed "Attention: Permissions Coordinator" to the address below.

Email: Info@opportunepublishing.com

Address: 113 N. Live Oak Street
Houston, TX 77003

CONTENTS

DEDICATION

This book is dedicated to every person who felt like they were misunderstood and alone. My kings and queens who may have thought that they weren't worthy. I want to remind all of you that you are unique and made to have an impact on the world with your story. Though I may not know you personally, just know that I see you and I love you. Yes, I said that I love you.

You deserve the world.

ACKNOWLEDGMENTS

This book is for my father; He passed away in 2020 and my world was turned upside down. I wanted to carry the legacy that he did not get to create when he was alive and writing a book was one of them. To my coach, Nikkie, thank you for believing in my dream and guiding me through this process. To my siblings, my mom, my family members and friends who have been such a support throughout my journey, I see all of you, I love you all and I am grateful. And to the highest, God, without you, I wouldn't have the strength to wake up every day and choose to smile. Thank you for keeping me, especially when I didn't want to keep myself.

Xiomara Bastien

CHAPTER 1
WHEN IT FEELS GOOD

Have you ever had a fantasy that came true?
This chapter emphasizes the lust that we feel when we meet someone new. The butterflies, the connections, the physical attraction, the sexy side of every love story.

This chapter introduces stories from different women, the people they have met, and what happens during the honeymoon phase. Sex with someone new is always exciting because you never know how it's going to be. But, the best sex you've had will always be engraved in your memory.

These poems illustrate the sexual encounters that these women would describe as the r "best". The many ways that they felt pleasure and how similar and different their stories are. Everyone is unique in their own ways. These poems show how women feel comfortable with their sexuality and how they would describe what they find sexually appealing.

Xiomara Bastien

The common ground behind these poems is that most women have a story, and no matter how they tell it, they all reminisce on how good it made them feel... at least in the moment.

Yazmine

I was newly single, and I wanted to finally forget.

My ex was still around, but he wasn't relevant and I didn't fret.

The same day I spoke to you, you were eager to come over.

And since I knew he wouldn't be home, I didn't want to wait any longer.

I slipped on something sexy that I knew would catch your eye.

But as we got comfortable, my ex unlocked the door, so I couldn't even lie.

I was explaining the situation to you, thinking it would chase you away, but it ended up turning you on.

So, as you passionately kissed every part of my upper body, I knew it was time to move on.

You couldn't wait to please me, so you pulled my panties down to kiss my second lips with your tongue. I was shaking and wanted to scream, but he was in the next room, and I was already sprung.

You made me weak when you were pleasuring me while we were both looking at the mirror.

You made me feel so good that for a second, I lost myself, and at the same time, I was able to see clearer.

I'll always have those memories of what you did to me.

And since we were both "single", I knew who to call and who I wanted to continue to see.

"You made me go through body changes more than once", you said; and I couldn't hide that smile because I knew then that your pleasure came from Me.

Arias

You were a Scorpio. I mean damn, do I really need to explain it?

You had me doing things that I would never see as a fit.

I remember the night you told me to walk around in just my heels as I pleased your eyes.

That didn't last long before you devoured me with positions that I could only fantasize.

Had me on counters while people were home, we could've gotten caught, but we didn't care.

You were able to awaken a hunger in me that the old Arias wouldn't dare.

I caught myself wanting you like a drug I never wanted to come off of.

You fed that desire that I only thought I'd see in movies and did it without a thought.

As much as I wanted to be good, you wouldn't even let me.

You knew exactly what to do to me, so that I opened up easily.

I caught myself thinking about your ways while you were away.

And I said to myself that no matter what, this is where I wanted to stay.

I felt sexy and wanted every time I was near you. I never wanted you to stop making me feel good.

As the good girl I used to be, you turned me into an alarm that woke up the entire neighborhood.

I want you nonstop and what people have to say has absolutely nothing to do with me.

I never thought that one person would have me act on everything I was feeling.

I wanted to experiment with you, sit on you, suck you and love you.

I always wanted more of you, and you had no problems making that desire come true.

Had me calling you daddy at times I didn't expect, and I knew that caught your attention.

Because you were telling me how much you're willing to be my interruption.

You're mine now, I hope you are fully aware of that.

Because I don't want to share this with any other person, you can believe that.

Carmen
The tale of two leos

Leo 1

You were younger, someone I didn't think would have this kind of impact on me.

I mean, how would I know that the way you kissed me would be to prepare me.

That same day, you turned my world inside out when your lips touched this p***y.

You worked your mouth the same way you kissed, and I couldn't wrap my mind around it.

Head game so strong, made me pull my own hair and baby, I didn't want you to quit it.

Just when I thought it couldn't get any better, you slid it in.

My mind was blown. I didn't think it was possible, but

it was just as good, so to me. you win.

I was addicted to how you handled me, so I had to have you more than once.

The many times you got into me never lacked anything, so I was gone thanks to you.

Leo 2

When I met you, I wasn't immediately convinced that you'd make much of a difference.

However, my attraction to you grew, and I was willing to take a chance.

You were my every day, consistent and reliable example of the man I said I wanted.

We could talk for hours, and you were the man that never left me stranded.

After the first kiss, something familiar came to mind, and I immediately knew you'd be a soul snatcher.

Unlike Leo 1, it took you longer to show me what I already knew would be a life-changer.

We were both willing and ready this time around, and when you reached the clit, I forgot all the promises I made.

You stopped, teased me, and told me you earned the cum on your face, warned me not to wipe it off, and I loved that game.

Being the rebel, I wiped it off, and daddy, you were willing to get your face dirty again.

Unlike many others, you switched up and took me to a place that I've never been.

I told you that this was it and that I didn't want you giving what was mine now to anyone else.

Every time was better than the last, and I was trying to figure out how you had me questioning everything else.

Marianne

What started out as friends going to dinner turned out to be one of my favorite memories.

A walk on the beach, sitting on top of you while you removed my top, gave me no worries.

I knew what it did to you when you invited me back to your place.

When you allowed me to lubricate my body for you to touch, I knew it was an open space.

You touched me with a mixture of softness and roughness, so I knew what would come after.

That hard body of yours didn't disappoint, especially knowing your d**k would be the same way; I gave you all the power.

The way you took over me had me grab your hand to choke me, to the point of short breaths.

And baby, I didn't mind it, as you could clearly depict

from my hardening breasts.

I commanded you to smack my ass; you did as you were told like a good boy.

I knew then that you could easily become my personal toy.

The embrace after we were done spoke volumes, and I realized that at that moment, I was spoiled.

Elena

You stood there, just as nervous as I was when we met in person for the first time.

You were so fine to me, and I got scared, wondering if you felt what I felt at the same time.

When I looked up at you, your eyes alone told me the words that I wanted to beg you to say aloud.

But you just hugged me and walked with me along the beach, which was our first route.

You had such a hunger for me that I could feel your body speaking for you when you grabbed me.

I wanted to feel everything with you and go somewhere where no eyes would see.

I felt like I knew you because of the safety you brought as you just held me.

My body was screaming for you, but I wanted you to work for it even when I was ready.

It's like you read my mind when you told me you had a hotel room for privacy.

I didn't care about anything else at that moment because this is what I've been wanting.

You didn't waste any time when you took my clothes off to see my body yearning.

You tasted me and told me that you'll be having me beg for it.

I knew then that you'd be a problem for me because I already needed a fix.

I let you do whatever you wanted to me and caught myself doing things I would usually avoid.

I begged for you many times, and you kept going, and it's a pleasure that my whole body enjoyed.

It's like you knew my body before that day because I didn't have to tell you what I liked for you to apply it.

I started asking myself stupid questions like "am I in love or addicted?"

Either way, I wanted you all the time, and every time, you had me at your service from the start.

I would never tell you, though, because I don't want you to think that you already had my heart.

You did me so right that I actually opened my mouth to call you "daddy".

Like wtf? I've never said that in my life. Why does this man have such a hold on me?

The nasty little words you whispered in my ear had me ready to risk it all.

But I had to remember that this is only the first time, so I had to make sure he'd call......

Bella

This man was so fine!!

Sexy, Latin, tall, full lips, an accent that would make anyone's body react.

I told myself that my challenge was to get you, so I had to interact.

I hit you with a pick-up line, and when you smiled and called me "mami", I knew it was a start.

You asked me for my number, and with no hesitation, I gave it to you, now that wasn't smart.

Opening that door with you, I knew it would be trouble because you physically checked the boxes.

I wanted to know everything about you fully without any roadblocks.

As things developed over time, I saw you in a completely different light.

You were gentle, affectionate, open, and this entire

time, not a single fight.

One night, after 3 months of love and passion, I wanted to do something we've never done before.

I got us things to play with and things that'll make us reach places where we would ask for an encore.

You tied my legs and arms to the bed; I was completely vulnerable.

But when you looked in my direction, I had to make myself accessible.

My body was your mouth's playground as you did not miss a single spot.

I wanted this to be endless because just thinking about it made me hot.

You told me that night that I was yours, and I completely believed you.

I came out to you and suggested that we watch something that would have us do something new.

As we watched, we explored, and when I tell you, I felt like my soul was leaving my body.

The longest night of my life that I never wanted to end became my favorite memory.

I knew what was possible for us to discover, and I

wanted you to continue to teach all these things to me.

Papi, dame lo que necesito y asi.

Ready?

Turn the red light on, and I know you're ready to show me exactly what I'm going to get.

I wore something black, skin-tight, and a pattern I knew you wouldn't forget.

Lingerie, barely covering the smooth skin you like to talk about so much.

I told you to sit in that chair, and the catch was that you couldn't touch.

I wanted you to study every inch and curve of my body so that you could create scenes.

Wrists tied together as you try to yank them off, so I started teasing you on my knees.

Pulling my body up slowly, as I come closer to your lips with mine.

I knew that I had you and that it was only a matter of time.

I decided to sit on your lap, facing you, and I couldn't resist anymore, so I kissed you.

It turned me on even more that you couldn't touch me, but you ended up breaking that too.

No more handcuffs restricting you from grabbing my body so passionately.

I felt weak, and I stopped thinking as I let myself go completely.

That lingerie never stood a chance to your hunger, and that, to me, was a turn on.

I've never experienced such passion, and I never hesitated. I was open.

The willingness that I had when you asked if you could blindfold me was a personal shock.

I never let go of control to where I would blindly trust, now I knew I was stuck.

You gave me goosebumps, and this time, there was nothing cold about them.

My body loved you before I even knew what I felt, I can't even describe it, damn...

When I covered my mouth to silently moan, you grabbed both hands and pinned them down.

Told me that you wanted to hear me and you were willing to drown.

You didn't stop until I came over and over again, as I begged you to stop.

Legs shaking, it felt like it fueled you to keep cleaning up, starting at the top.

As I got louder, you had to turn the music up to avoid your neighbors.

But I knew that our music and the speakers would only make things worse.

I wanted every inch of you, and I had no problem expressing it to you.

We were on the same page, and over time, my desire for you only grew.

The intensity intertwined with the gentle passion was unlike anything I've had.

It's when you knew what to do without even asking, and you reached that spot.

I know this isn't official, but this isn't something that I'm willing to share.

I wasn't ready for all that I got from you, I know it's new, but I don't care. I wasn't ready for all of that; it started as a dare.

All I wanted

I didn't want anything to become serious.

The attraction was there, and I was curious.

I didn't want anything to go tc too high of a level.

But that chemistry was messing with my mind.

You spoke certain words to me that had me ready.

But all I wanted was for you to apply your mouth down there and remain steady.

I didn't want to go all the way, but I wanted to put your money where your mouth was.

So I teased you to the point when I didn't even ask; the choice was yours.

You wanted to bring me pleasure.

And even when I warned you that I wouldn't have sex, you wanted to find my treasure.

You listened to every inch of my body and knew what spot to hit while you ate.

And I had to let my head fold back as I became a clean slate.

All I wanted was to know your lips' language, nothing more.

And now I'm ready to go to sleep, my legs are sore. No sex remember?

I wasn't lying when I said it.

So I hope that the snippet you got was all that you needed.

Paradise

We felt the same way.

We just weren't aware.

Conversation was effortless.

What I wanted between us was there.

The way you spoke to me.

The way you looked at me.

I knew there had to be desire.

I wanted you to say something first.

I knew if I asked you questions, I'd find out.

As we got more comfortable.

You opened up.

We connected.

And you admitted.

That was a feeling that made my body react.

Not only was it physical.

You stimulated my mind.

Every single word was that of a man.

The maturity and communication had me finished.

I wanted you so bad.

I wanted to do things to you that I used to be shy about.

I wanted to see what you were capable of.

And you didn't waste any time.

Just kissing you, alone, was passion.

The way you grabbed me was ecstasy.

You sent goosebumps all through my body without even penetrating me.

That's when I knew how the sex would be.

I forgot that I was shy the moment you kissed it.

You ate it like you'd been waiting for that moment.

I don't know how many times I erupted.

When I tried to run away, you wouldn't let me.

You kept wanting to please me.

I couldn't deny how much that turned me on.

So I was ready.

I returned the favor.

And I was glad that I got to see what you had.

It was perfect.

And I knew exactly what to do with it.

As I heard you moaning, I didn't want to stop.

I wanted you to feel what you made me feel.

And baby, it felt good.

You were ready and wouldn't let me finish.

As you went in, you grabbed my neck.

How did you know I liked that?

Communication was definitely key.

I loved the fact that you askec for feedback.

You got me hooked.

It only took one time for me to know that I was addicted.

Sammy

I don't want to work too much.

I just want you to undress me, and let's go.

It's clear that we both want each other, so why wait?

We've known each other long enough for me to know you don't play.

I don't want to keep wondering, "what if?"

So, show me how you apply your words to your actions.

You knew immediately that I didn't like it slow.

That I wanted you to make me beg for more.

The way you grabbed my body woke me up.

I felt like it was a necessity to keep you strong.

You took me with hunger, and I wanted it all.

I did as I was told every time with no regrets.

You have no idea how turned on I was when you flipped me.

I felt light, and baby, I didn't want you to stop.

I wanted to let you let me do you too.

I climbed on top of you and showed you why they call it riding.

I got you to say my name, and I felt good about it.

You grabbed my thighs so tight I felt every inch of my body tighten.

It felt so good, and I knew to you it was the same.

I kept going, slowly, even after you came.

Hearing you call me "baby" solidified what I was feeling.

So, I knew there would be more opportunities where we wouldn't be speaking.

Xiomara Bastien

CHAPTER 2
THE AFTERMATH

What happened after that unforgettable night?

Chapter 2 highlights the aftermath of what happens after you have what most would call "the best I've ever had". Did the relationship grow into what you wanted or expected? Did he call you the next day? Or did he walk away from you when you least expected it?

Sometimes what feels good at the moment doesn't always bring a happy ending, and sometimes it does. However, we will never know until we do. These women explain the different experiences that they've had after what should've been an amazing memory.

This chapter is here to show men and women that they're not alone; some stories are similar, others are unexpected. What comes after a great moment is when reality hits, feelings may get involved, and people are not always on the same page.
This is the aftermath.

Yazmine

We were both single, right?

At least that's what you told me.

Turns out, you were still with her and used me.

You wanted to get back at her for something that you didn't even know was an actual fact.

You let your suspicions turn into impulsion and didn't know how to act.

You didn't even give me the option of saying yes or no.

I was open with you about my situation, and you couldn't even let me know.

I didn't expect a relationship out of this just so you know.

I just wanted something that I didn't have to hide or do on the low.

I hope that using me for your own pleasure worked out for you.

Because that's a pleasure I needed at the time, and I'm ok with us being through.

I'll never respect you for the way you went about things.

But I can thank you for giving me a simple moment of bliss.

Carmen
The tale of two leos

Leo 1

It was sometime later that I realized it wasn't the same. Maybe it was so much time passed, but there was no walk of shame this time around.

Yes, it was good, but the chemistry that once existed was not there.

What you did to me in the past wasn't present, which to me was unfair.

That night wasn't enough for me, and I definitely wanted more of you.

But you started acting differently, and I had a feeling that my request wouldn't come through.

As more time went by, I moved on to another and had a son.

You popped back up, I was in a different place and my feelings for you were none.

You had the chance to be the man who made me feel things I only watched women talk about in movies.

But you didn't know what you wanted, so I got someone who knew how to shut down my insecurities.

Leo 2

It was short-lived, what I thought that we would be changed the day you got that call.

I knew it was her. What I suspected was what happened, and I questioned why I had to fall.

You immediately shot me when you pulled the trigger that she was pregnant and that you'd try to work it out.

You brought out something in me that I promised myself would never come out.

And I knew the only way to stop being near you or talk to you was to cut you off completely.

I'll keep this short when I say that you were everything I wanted and didn't at the same time, but you were also able to teach me...

That you were on borrowed time with me and that I wasn't the woman for you.

And that no matter what I would've done, I wouldn't be a priority to you.

It's funny because the one I didn't think anything of

initially was the same one to give me a unique ending.

You were a weakness that I allowed in my space even when it was just you; that's all you ever needed to bring.

Marianne

Nights and days went by, but you've been on my mind heavily lately.

I have no idea why I wanted that night we had, to happen daily.

The cliché response would be that I was "falling in love with my friend after crossing the line".

It wasn't just that, I know that souls tie, but you had my body screaming for yours on mine.

I called one night, and he sounded different and said that we had to talk.

I didn't know what to expect, but for some reason, I got happy, until you didn't let me inside, and I asked that we took a walk.

My heart was beating out of my chest, wondering if you would end it all before I told you how I felt.

You paused and looked at me and told me that I am

a woman who should be kept.

I got excited, but you shut that down right away by saying that you aren't the one I should be kept by.

Mentioning that we should still be friends and that you'd always be there when I wanted to be high.

I was disappointed and immediately knew that I was just one of your many options.

I mean, what did I expect, right? A man to get what he wanted and stick around with good intentions?

I think I'm good on you and will continue to keep my distance.

Just stay away from me, because I know if you come over, things will get intense.

Elena

Wow, for the first time, I can say that I'm truly speechless.

I thought this would be something great, but this whole damn thing is a mess.

Time went by, as we actually started to say we were in a relationship.

I never felt such an attraction to someone in such a short period, s**t!

I fell for who you pretended to be when you could've just been honest.

I get that sometimes it's too good and that you still want others while keeping me.

But seeing you with someone publicly while you claimed I was the only one, f****d me up.

I started asking myself what I ever did wrong, all while filling up my cup.

I texted you that I wanted to talk about something surprising, and you didn't suspect a thing.

As you came over and walked in, I told you that I wanted to show you something.

There they were, in a gift bag, all of the pictures of them that I got from that day in the resort.

My meeting with my investor for your business ended early, which was the blessing given to me to report.

You begged me not to leave you and that she didn't mean anything.

So, I told you to call her on facetime to let her know that she was nothing.

Yet, I still made sure we were no longer a thing.

Bella

In my mind, I thought we would never have an expiration date.

Here I was, ring on my finger, and walking down the aisle to my soulmate.

Tears flowed down your face when my father walked me to my forever.

Three years together, obstacles and endless love, anything negative was always a "never".

Since the day I met you, I knew that you would be a problem for me and that you were the one.

You showed me the world through different lenses, and after you, I knew there would be none.

After a year of being married, things were starting to get tough.

I couldn't see you for days as you claimed that you were away for work, and it was rough.

I believed you for a while, but something did not sit right with me, especially when you came home and gave me no attention.

I felt like every time we were near one another, I had to beg for your affection.

You were my heart, twin flame, other half, so I knew you were doing something behind my back.

So, one day, I followed you, knowing I was going to catch you with her and I would not give you any slack.

What I found out was worse.

I was going to lose my best friend, and you've been hurting this entire time alone.

It was a tumor, and you didn't want to tell me because if I cried, you wouldn't be able to live with yourself.

I much would have rather you cheat on me than die on me.

All the talks we had about being together for 40 more years and starting a family.

I was on the ground, praying to God that this man never leaves my side.

It was too late, you were gone a week later, and I lost the whole fight.

You were everything to me, and I lost everything when you left me.

I've cried rivers of tears and sorrow in your memory.

I don't think I'll ever love another the way I felt with you.

And that's ok because I will love our son with as much love, if not more, in honor of you.

Arias

Toxic.

The kind of relationship that would usually make me sick.

Looking back now, I know that I should've listened to my own advice.

Where I would tell my friends to ignore the "men" who tried to play them, like dice.

I chose to stay despite the many times you instilled fear in me.

I knew I deserved better, but even with my eyes wide open, I couldn't see.

The disrespect, the subtle threats and constant frustration made me want to forget.

That even when I knew you were no good for me, I couldn't really regret.

I remember the day I no longer felt safe with you like it was yesterday.

You thought that I would be the one who would set you up with your friends, so on the road, I had to pray.

I thought I'd lose my life that day when you took me to the woods, and I knew you had a gun.

I knew that I deserved better, and I knew that I had to take the option to run.

I no longer felt safe in your space.

My first love, my first everything, I never wanted to lose sight of my own pace.

But going by what you wanted, I don't think this is what I wanted anymore.

I deserve a man who would treat me like a queen and show me the meaning of adore.

I didn't want to be another memory for you because my love for you surpassed all your flaws.

So, I stayed, wishing and praying that who you said you were was worth my life being put on pause.

Eventually, I became strong enough to walk away from the man I thought would always be. But I discovered who I was when I decided that the smile on my face depended only on me.

Terrified

What just happened?

This wasn't just any sex with any man; it was with you.

You studied my body like it was something you already knew.

I got scared when something unexpected happened.

You didn't run away like I thought this story would've shortened.

You wanted to stick around and have a future with me.

I didn't know how to respond to it, so I decided that it was too good to be.

You were everything that I said I needed and wanted in a life partner.

But I'm so used to being used that I didn't want this to be another dagger.

I was terrified to be loved by you because I knew that

if it ended, I would be devastated.

I made things up in my mind like they were the ones you stated.

I can't love you the way that you deserve to be.

So, I don't know if this is something that you're willing to see.

I have so many sides that even scare me.

Can you love me past all of that?

Addicted

You had me wrapped around your fingers.

There was never a time that I didn't want to be there.

I caught myself smiling at the thought of you.

So, I had to be the one to ask you.

I didn't know if it was lust or love because it felt like both.

The chemistry, the laughs and deep conversations brought us close.

But is it too good to be true?

Are you the man who knows what to do?

I've been going over this in my mind a thousand times.

Wondering if it's something worth talking about at all.

I thought I knew what I wanted until you started changing

my perspective.

Had me wondering why I should ever reject it.

You had me under your spell so many times that I lost my words.

Because once we lay down, communication is worse.

You make me want to take chances, but I'm not sure I want to right now.

You want more, and the rules are reversed now.

As the woman, I should be the one who's holding it down.

But you want more.

And I don't know if that's something that I have in me anymore.

Wasted Energy

It was like nothing I've ever had.

The passion.

The sex.

The conversation.

The mutual respect.

I couldn't get enough of you.

And I've tried talking myself out of it.

It was weird how comfortable we got so fast.

I didn't believe how you felt about me.

It was too good to be true.

I told myself so many times.

But you never changed.

You made me want to take risks.

You were one of the only ones to get me to let my guard down.

So why was I so skeptical?

The way you spoke to me got me annoyed.

It was so sweet and was pure poetry.

Therefore, I couldn't believe a word.

You were consistent and always checked on me.

But I still doubted.

And then it dawned on me.

I've never had exactly what I asked for.

And now that I had it, I didn't know how to handle it.

I tried pulling back, but you wouldn't let me.

You called me out on my s**t, and that was necessary.

How did I get so lucky?

Things remained the same over time.

But we had a secret.

And that was one that I knew I couldn't live with.

You wanted me to lie for you.

At first, I did.

But then I realized that this isn't me.

You were perfect everywhere else, but this consumed me.

I had to leave you behind even when it hurt me.

I wish you understood me.

I can't keep or be that secret.

And the fact that you didn't fight for me cleared it.

I want to walk away, but my heart won't let me.

This time though, I won't listen to it.

Because when I ignore my intuition and God, I end up in a pit.

I get to separate myself from the lust and open my eyes.

Because I don't want it to take years for me to realize.

Sammy

You didn't have a choice.

With the way I made you feel, I knew a ring would follow.

I loved the way you asked me.

Since you knew I was unconventional.

My favorite song in the background.

You shirtless.

No flowers.

Just my favorite candles.

I just thought you were romantic.

I had no idea what was coming.

You didn't even get down on one knee.

So, in my mind, we were both about to be happy.

But then you looked down, in my eyes.

And asked, "what are your plans for the rest of your life?"

I was confused.

And I was about to list them to you.

But you stopped me.

And you wouldn't stop staring at me.

So, I asked what was wrong.

And you said, "Nothing, I'm just wondering if you'd want to spend it with me."

I still didn't understand.

Then you reassured me when you said: "will you please marry me?"

Attitude and all, I gladly said yes, because there's no other man who's I'd be.

Xiomara Bastien

CHAPTER 3
QUESTIONS

What happens if they walk away?

Did you end up together?

Or would you categorize them as unfit?

Chapter 3 addresses the thoughts that we carry around with us on a daily basis. Whether positive or negative, we constantly ask ourselves questions that we're too afraid to express out loud. How did we really feel?

Did we tell them how we really felt?

Do we have any regrets?

These poems show the human side of every question we ask ourselves. They show everyone reading that they're not alone when these thoughts cross their minds. That it is okay to have unanswered questions and to want closure even when they know what the silence means.

This chapter is for every single person who has ever felt as though they weren't good enough, or too good, or questioning their feelings and emotions; you are human.

What questions do you ask yourself?

Am I Good Enough?

I often wonder why I always ended up getting ghosted by men I am willing to be with.

I mean, I'm exactly what he's described as the woman he wanted to end up with.

I guess words were just that, and I am not the girl that he will ever want.

Am I good enough?

I always end up questioning my value when they end up leaving, and I don't.

I'm the one who puts in all the effort, and I never end up with even half of what I give.

I end up hurt in the end, and I know that's not a way to live.

Am I enough?

Do these men actually find me attractive, or should I

book my body-altering surgery?

Is it my hair? Is my ass big enough? Did they find someone better to fulfill their needs?

My mind is racing, and my heart is pounding at the thought that I might end up alone.

But I realized that it's better to be alone while waiting for the one who wouldn't steer you wrong.

I hope that I can convince myself that I am good enough for someone to love.

I have so much love to give and no one to receive what I was initially scared of.

It's been years since I last decided that I want to love and be loved again, and I know now that I am ready.

I no longer want to rush into the temporary idea of forever and get attached too quickly.

I am focusing on loving the one person that I never took the time to appreciate, me.

The one person I can count on to push, uplift and cherish me is me.

I've wasted so much time on men who didn't value me, but I woke up and looked in the mirror at a woman who is worthy.

These "boys" pretended to have emotions and feelings when they had other intentions.

I let them use me and promised myself that there wouldn't be any emotions.

But I've lied to myself so many times that I ended up falling every single time.

I may not be the most attractive woman in the world, but I know that I'm worth this crime.

The one called love that we all seem to have an allergic reaction to.

But that we chase blindly, ignoring the obvious signs just like we usually do.

Am I good enough?

A question that I constantly ask myself, knowing that I deserve better.

Was It Me?

Did I say something for you to ignore me?

Did I hit a nerve with you that maybe I didn't see?

I feel guilty for what I don't even know that I might've done.

I question the number of times I did the same thing to you. Maybe that's why you're gone.

I wonder if it was the way that I loved you, or how I touched you or how I opened up to you.

Did I go too deep into who I was too early, and that scared you?

I remember just being there, sitting with you and held you when you were stressed.

I wanted to show you that it's you that God has blessed.

I wanted you to know that even when you're hurting, I'd never leave.

Maybe that's what scared you away; maybe you felt like it was too good, so it had to be a dream.

I was willing to love you past your pain, and heal with you in the process.

But you didn't give me a chance to have a vision of the progress.

Was it me?

Did I not start enough arguments because I just wanted to cuddle?

Was it that I was scared to tell you I loved you and you saw me struggle?

I fell hard for you, and it all happened when you wanted to start pursuing.

Did I move too fast when you said you wanted to be with me and that this was a forever thing?

Was it my body that chased you away?

Did it not satisfy your pleasures and make your day?

I'm sorry. All I wanted was a love deeper than the puddles that I walk passed in the morning.

One that surpassed any obstacle or challenge because to us, it's everything.

Maybe I was too much and said too much that made you feel like this was too good to be true.

Maybe it was the fact that I didn't want anything from you, and I just wanted you.

I mean, were any of these moments real to you like they were to me?

Or was I the only one who felt the love that would eventually bring me to my knees?

I wish I had the answers and that I wouldn't have to ask. But your disappearance woke something up in me, and I don't want to repeat the same task.

I need to know where I f****d up so that I don't put the next through what I did to you.

So please let me know if I was too much when I just wanted to love you.

I need to know if healthy and genuine love is something you're allergic to.

So that the next man who deserves it receives that love and cherishes it too.

Was it me?

Or all of this uncertainty, sadness and toxicity coming from you?

Can You Handle Me?

I have to tell you.

I'm not one of those easy girs who are quick to get into.

Can you come correct when you approach me?

I don't want another little boy telling me how sexy I am or how much he wants me.

You want to impress me?

Stop handing me your words and start showing me.

I hope you know that I'm worth it, so this won't be something that a few words can get to.

Can you answer any questions about me when others ask you?

Can you handle me?

Because I'm not a little girl begging for someone else's

attention.

I'm a woman who wants a man who will willingly and voluntarily give me affection.

Can you hold me when I'm having an anxiety attack and talk me through it?

Can you love me even when you're angry, or will you just quit?

Can you handle me?

Will you be there for me and communicate with me when it gets hard, or will you run away?

Do you deserve for me to open my heart to you when you know you're not going to stay?

Can you handle me?

I know when I first asked you, you made up your mind that I meant it sexually.

But, the fact is, most people would be able to physically.

Can you fulfill the needs I have mentally, spiritually, and respectfully?

I mean, if not, then why are you standing here to waste my time?

You can have any other girl, right? So why are you still

in front of me with rhymes?

I guess that's a question you've never been asked before because you want a girl, not a woman.

And it's okay to want that, but I am not the one you're looking for fam.

I have depths in my body and my mind that I haven't reached yet; would you reach them with me?

Would you want to explore every inch of my body before you even undress me?

Can you handle me?

Sometimes I'm in my own world, and don't want to be bothered.

Would you stick around? Or would you add me to the list of those you conquered?

Can you handle me?

If you don't want all of me, including my insecurities, my pain, my heart, my smile and even my sorrows, you can walk out that door.

I won't be the woman who sticks around for "men" who don't put in effort, consistency and respect anymore.

Your silence doesn't surprise me. Because the fact is we both knew you couldn't handle me.

Who's Getting Used? (Him)

Phone rings.

Today, I want you around, but don't ask me about the other days.

Let's enjoy the moment we're having right now before it's too late.

I call you when I want that type of girlfriend vibe that's still not official.

I want to laugh with you while we play video games but still, no pressure.

You call me for the same, except you want free smoking sessions.

I don't mind that because our situation comes with different sections.

With you by my side, I don't think it's something I can have with another girl.

But I would never tell you that, even when I love everything about you, down to the last curl.

I have to remember, though, instead of communicating, I will assume that you're talking to another man.

And I know you think the same way that I do, and even if you don't, you're a smart woman.

I like when I call you on the phone, and you say "hey baby", in your sleepy voice.

But I'll never tell you that so you don't think that I'm too thirsty.

I'll keep playing it cool while I hold you, so you don't see me as weak.

I know you use me when you come over and say you "need a friend right now".

You knew how horny I was, you teased me, and here I am, here and now.

I'll never tell you, but when I'm physically connecting with them, I'm with you mentally.

I like the trips you take me on with your knowledge and way of thinking.

I remember my mom asking me what I wanted and needed in a woman, and I realized that all of the things that I listed, you had.

So, I tried to talk myself out of it because I knew that I didn't deserve even half of that.

I wanted not to trust you, despite the fact that you were always honest, even when it hurt.

I wanted to start an argument just to make you see that it wasn't all good, I had to put you on alert.

But you stayed, friends with benefits, and you got me feeling things that I'm avoiding.

Things I desperately want to express, but I can't because I don't want us expiring.

I'd rather suffer with myself than tell you that I love you. We were using each other, so it became harder and harder to walk away from you.

I'd rather be the shoulder to cry on than be the one to hurt you.

And I know if I tell you how I feel, there's a possibility that my dream to have you won't come true.

I think today's the day that I decide to risk it all by telling you.

Because I know that even when I think I'm not ready, I will dedicate the time needed to make you mine one day.

Phone rings.

Her: "Hey, I was just thinking about you, that's crazy, you barely ever call though, are you okay?"

My palms are sweating, but I have to play it cool, so she doesn't feel it.

It's time to tell her to come over to talk and hang out; this is it.

Me: "Hey, can you come over tonight? I want to talk to you about something."

Her: "Yeah, I can, what time?"

Me: "I wish you could just come now."

Her: "I'm on my way."

I thought I was about to pass out. She only lives 10 minutes away.

I took a shot to get loose, man I think I need to pray.

She pulls up, and I run out to her because I couldn't wait anymore.

I poured my heart out, which shocked me too, s**t, it felt like I had to do a chore.

By the time I was done, with tears in my eyes, she couldn't look at me.

When she finally looked up, I melted when she said, "I

was wondering when you were going to feel the same about me."

This is the woman that I deserve to marry, and what I didn't expect ended up happening.

No regrets, who's using who? Maybe I used you more, but you ended up being everything.

Why'd You Break Me?

I have so many questions for you when we finally meet.

You fed me lies and then apologize before I could even speak.

All these years, I put my blood, sweat, and tears into what I thought was a relationship.

Just to find out that to you, I was the girl you'd keep using, and I wouldn't trip.

Seeing her pictures on your phone wasn't even the best part.

It's the fact that you thought I wouldn't notice what you called your "piece of art".

I tried to wrap my mind around the many times you told me you'd marry me.

But come to think of it, they were unkept promises that were never made complete.

I tried to remind myself of who I am, but I completely forgot who she is.

Because the old me wouldn't have stood there in disbelief of your betrayal, " I thought I was his".

Four months pregnant with an engagement ring that should've been thrown away.

And here you were, in my bed, with my sister, when you claimed you had a busy day.

I always wondered why you and my sister hated each other as much as you did.

Now at least one question was answered; I just wish that who I was carrying wasn't your kid.

For a second, I thought that maybe I would be happy with a man again.

But I was wrong; I don't think I'll ever recover from this pain.

I wish I knew what made him go to those extremes. Did he hate me?

I gave him everything he ever wanted, and this is how he treats me?

I walked out, grabbed my keys, and ran to my car while blocking him out.

I drove off, tears welling up my eyes as I headed to my best friend's house.

As I explained the story to her, she didn't have much to say.

She told me that after what I told her, that I should probably stay.

Confused and angry, I wanted to know what other secrets weren't told to me.

She explained that my sister may be another one who's carrying your baby.

I was done, and with rage, I drove back home, and to my surprise, she wasn't gone.

I grabbed your clothes from the drawers, you couldn't even stop me; i grew cold.

I set fire to your s**t since you want to be cool, let me put some heat in your life.

Why'd you break me?

Having me out here showing people the real meaning of crazy.

It's funny how the ones breaking you are the same ones pointing the finger at you so that others can see.

Why Do You Want Me?

I keep asking myself over and over again why you want me.

I'm stubborn, emotional and I require a lot of attention, so why me?

I know for a fact that I don't have the best body, and I'm not as attractive as these other women.

You can have whoever you want, but I'm the one who you wanted to let in.

You were willing to let me know who you were and openly admitted it.

But how come when your ex was around, you couldn't give her answers that fit.

I may be trippin', but I wondered why so many times.

Why, out of every woman you came across, I'm the one that gave you a sign.

I don't think I deserve a man who looks as good as you do.

I don't see myself being the trophy wife for a man like you.

So, I'll ask again, why do you want me?

I've seen the attention that you get, and you always seem to just brush it off.

And here I am, next to you, regular clothes, no makeup and sweats, how are you not turned off?

It seems as though the more tme you spend with me, the more your love keeps growing.

But out of fear, I always end up being the one running.

I started asking myself if you're using me.

I've never been with someone who truly showed me what it was like to feel loved.

To feel like you have nothing to worry about and that your feelings don't have to be shoved...

In the back of your mind, you feel like something has to be wrong.

This right here is too good to be true, so I tried to play strong.

Like I wasn't falling more in love with you each time you're around.

And when you're away, I'm ready to ask you to come back for another round.

You make me want to let go of my insecurities and love you fully.

That scares me because every time I did, I ended up heartbroken, completely.

But, you, you make me feel levels of love that I've never experienced before.

Patience that accepts me for me, and I must say I want you more.

So, why me?

When did you decided that I was the one you wanted to give what you've never given to others?

I wish I could answer my own questions, but for the first time, I don't have any worries, and that's all that matters.

Am I A Player?

Guy 1: you were amazing in bed, but your conversation was flat, so I'll keep you for what you're good at.

Guy 2: you stimulate me mentally, and that's sexy to me, you're the only one who can do that.

Guy 3: I love our fancy dates and your immediate ways of taking me on trips.

Guy 4: I will have to let you go because of your lack of consistency.

Call it what you want, but I know I need more than one to fulfill me.

They each get their time, and I get what I want when necessary.

No, they don't all get some, but guy 1, he holds my lower heartbeat.

The rest of them know it's not on the table; they have their own responsibilities.

I don't really care what others have to say about my situation.

I love that I can be me and do what I want without hesitation.

I'm clear and honest with all of them so that there is no miscommunication.

Before you say anything, go try it yourself, sis.

And maybe you'll come back and tell me that your old life is not what you miss.

I'll help you get what you want if you need this.

But before you judge what I'm doing, look at yourself and ask, "Am I able to be a player like she is?"

My Mistake?

How can such a pleasure become such a turnoff.

Believing the words that didn't have actions to match should've been the warning.

But deciding to go with it and ignore my intuition was not befitting.

I wanted to give you the benefit of the doubt and figure things out on my own.

Yet, I should've gone with my gut and put myself first before you were gone.

Was it my mistake?

To feel something so strong despite the fact that I knew it would be toxic?

To give so much of myself when I knew that I wouldn't be the one you'd pick?

To make the first move as you pretended to be shy

when in reality you knew what you were doing?

I mean, was it all me?

Did I not realize that what you really wanted was to make a longer listing?

I wish I knew.

Or maybe I did.

Why didn't I listen to that little voice telling me that you were a grown kid?

I saw the signs, but I guess I had the superpowers to change you.

I'll take the blame this time because I went against what I already knew.

You Love Me?

I'll never understand why it's so easy for people to say that they love you.

I mean, how do you really know that it's love when the only thing you know is the view?

I can't believe a word you say when you barely know anything about me.

I can't take you seriously when you keep blurting these complex words to me.

Can you tell me what my favorite color or what my middle name is?

Can my family trust you to keep me safe so that I don't have to ball up my fists?

How can you love me when you haven't seen me at my worse?

What makes you think that it's something that you can live with, especially when I curse.

I don't want to have to change myself because of your idea of who I am.

I don't want to have to change who I am based on your expectations.

I am cold, and sometimes I wonder if I can completely love again.

You're this man, who on paper is perfect, but what are you hiding that I may not be able to stand?

I can't tell you that I feel the same way when I barely even know you.

And it's clear that I'm not one of those girls who will fall all over you.

Your looks may get you through the door, but the man you really are is still a mystery.

I notice the little things, and it seems like your story needs way more of a recovery.

Your stories don't always add up.

And sometimes, when your friends say something that you've done, you switch up.

It's a challenge to ignore details that can make or break something that might've been real.

And it's also a challenge to find a quick way to change

how you feel.

I don't love you back because I know I need to know and accept more.

And I don't know if I'm willing to stick around for what's in store.

I remember asking you a question, and you ended up lying.

I didn't forget about that, no matter how hard I was trying.

I can't love someone entirely when I already have my doubts.

What do I do?

Do I go with it and ignore the signs, or do I go back to being one of the scouts?

Am I Allowed?

Am I allowed to hug you when you cry?

Should I give you space when you ask for it?

Am I allowed to show you I want you by touching your thigh?

Or should I hold back and wait for you to make the first move?

Am I allowed to show interest in your dreams and your aspirations?

Because I want to know and support you to your destination.

Am I allowed to hold you when you feel stressed?

Or should I leave you alone with your thoughts?

I'm not sure what to do because even when I ask, you never respond.

So, am I allowed to leave?

When you've made it clear that you don't want me around.

Or should I work harder to get you to loosen up and come around?

Am I allowed to love you?

Because I'm ready to do it, but if you don't want me to, I'll find someone else to give it to.

Are You Ok?

I've seen you many times.

Sitting alone and studying each street line.

You seemed far away.

Like, the only present thing in you was your body.

I can tell that your mind was elsewhere.

That you wanted to stay alone, anywhere.

I could see the pain in your eyes when you glanced at me.

And I felt it when you looked away just as quickly.

I wanted to run after you, but you didn't know me.

So, I prayed that whatever you were going through didn't consume you.

I had a "f**k it" moment and ran anyway because that

was a look that I knew.

When I finally reached you, it's like you were relieved.

That someone was able to see you before you took a leap.

You introduced yourself as if you knew I would come to you.

And when I heard your name was the same as mine, I felt it too.

I was meant to meet you because it was like meeting my old self.

And as I continued to speak to you, I knew that I had made the right decision.

My conversation with you changed both of our lives.

And I didn't realize until now that everyone needs someone sometimes.

CHAPTER 4
LESSON LEARNED?

Did you learn your lesson the first time, or did you have to make it a few times?

Chapter 4 lists the many ways that human beings either leave old habits behind, are addicted to them, or find themselves stuck in the middle. Many people learn from their mistakes and make a decision to change their patterns. Others have a hard time accepting that someone they fall for may not want the same thing, and they keep going back.

Did you grow from that toxic relationship? Or did they ruin an entire gender because of you? How do you feel about leading someone on? Do you think they're stupid for believing a word you say?

Chapter 4 is a combination of men's and women's lessons from their past experiences. Were they able to grow from those situations, or did they keep repeating the same patterns they were used to?

CAUTION: this chapter may be a little savage.

Hurt People

Healed.

I remember the days when I told myself that I deserved what I got.

The screaming, the abuse, the lies, the cheating, you know, the type of s**t that'll make your heart stop.

Broken for years, I chased "men", especially when they had me doing all the work.

Those were my favorites, no calls or "good morning" texts; I guess the thoughts going through my mind were a perk.

I knew you weren't right for me, which is why I thought that these others would somehow heal me.

I guess we all have dumb moments, and I had a couple, clearly.

No matter what I did, you never left my mind, which made me start to wonder why.

I never completely forgave you or myself for the waste of my time.

Looking back now, I needed what I had with you because I would've never found myself the way I did. I was told that hurt people, hurt people, and for the longest time, I never understood it.

It's clear that you never received a love like mine, and it was the kind that didn't want anything in return.

Yours was different. Even when you felt it, you'd rather watch it burn.

No matter what, I stayed with you to prove to you that I would never hurt you.

But you didn't trust me, and no matter what I said and even showed, it was never enough for you.

Things have changed now, especially after running into you randomly.

When I saw you after 2 full years, I didn't feel anything but pity.

I felt bad for who taught you how to love.

For them to teach you to hurt before you got hurt.

You weren't the same, and I knew it by the look in your eyes.

I couldn't say yes to your proposition because I was no longer blind.

I fought hard these past two years to fully feel the love I do for myself.

And I was willing to help you find the same, but I wouldn't be there for it.

I wish you knew how deserving you are and how much love you have in you to give.

However, it is no longer my job to open you up to what life really is.

I had to make sure that you were okay and that you had a place to stay.

She kicked you out of your place and called the police, so you had to run away.

God works in mysterious ways and made it so that I could see what came of your life.

And the same one who you left me for became the one that had no problems twisting that knife.

The irony is, that would've been me, so God, I thank you for taking me away from this strife.

Who Wants To Get Played? (Him)

It's crazy when the player gets played, right?

I did what I had to do so that she wouldn't get close.

But it was impossible to do that as soon as she got a dose.

I've broken so many hearts that it became fun for me.

So when I met you, I caught myself trying to change how I should be.

I didn't like it, I didn't like the fact that you understood me.

That when something was wrong, you noticed, and I didn't even have to speak.

I always try to keep my head and my heart separately because of situations like this.

I started questioning myself when I got happy with a simple kiss.

Like shorty, you know what I want, why do you keep playing with me?

Making me feel s**t that I swore I wouldn't, am I going crazy?

I caught myself thinking about you when you weren't around, and that scared me.

I wanted to tell you how I felt, but that's a side that I didn't want you to see.

I was never taught how to be soft, and I never wanted to be broken like I broke those other women.

So I had to hide, play around and being able to conquer them was a win.

There was no other way to word this besides the fact that I'm afraid of karma.

I was ready to walk away as soon as I felt something to somehow avoid the future drama.

Yes, I said future, because that part always comes in a relationship, and I don't want that.

Say what you want, but I've seen my mom enough to know that love is not a fact.

I've watched her get mistreated by "men" who claimed that they loved her.

WE HAVE MANY SIDES, WHAT'S YOURS?

And they would end up doing the exact opposite and leave her alone with her emotions to transfer.

How can I love you when I don't even know who I am so I can love myself?

Can you answer that question, love? Or is this situation all about yourself?

I always end up convincing someone that I have feelings when I really didn't.

Now it's the other way around, where I wish you knew so that I didn't have to let you in.

But now that I know what kind of girl you are, I'm about to fall back.

Because even though I didn't tell you, you shouldn't have taken him back.

I hated the feeling that someone would hurt and not tell me why.

Come to think of it, maybe that's why I made so many others cry.

Instead of taking responsibility for not telling you how I felt, I'll put the blame on you.

Now, who's next? Who's willing to be with me and see what we can get into?

Short And Sweet

Yes, I lied. But it's your fault for believing me.

How could you not see that all I wanted to do was f**k?

You caught feelings when I warned you not to, so it's not my fault.

I told you I didn't want to be in a relationship even though I treated you like we were.

I would've done anything if it was going to get me there.

I got all the information out of you so that I could use it to my advantage.

You were a nice girl, so I felt bad for a minute, but it became your turn, so "center stage".

I liked everything you did to me and for me, but baby, your feelings don't matter to me.

I knew that if I told you what you loved to hear, I would end up getting you for free.

Call it what you want, I call this whole situation "smart".

Because I don't have to be like these weak dudes out here with a heart.

Stop calling my phone baby, I ghosted you.

It's been two weeks now. By now, you should get the clue.

I'm going to be like this until my very dying day.

The way I've been with you was great, but it's not in my blood to stay.

I hope you find what you're looking for, you could've been a good one.

But I don't care to find out, I'm gone.

Blocked

I never thought that it would come to this.

What happened?

We were good, so good that you're the one who wanted to go through with it.

You initiated a relationship you knew you weren't ready for.

I thought I knew you, but I guess I only saw the side that was far from the core.

You had me falling hard, ready to risk it all and see what's in store.

For me, this was it, the final chapter of my many failed relationships.

Now we're strangers, and it's time to take different ships.

I didn't deserve the disappearance, and I know it wasn't

me.

So it's time to be done, time to again choose me.

Now, you will no longer have access to me.

It's time to block and block out the ones who no longer serve me.

Untitled

We're scared.

I thought that I was the only one hurting, but it seems like you are too.

I wish I knew how to ask you what it was without feeling like I was bothering you.

Our thought process is to run away from others when we feel ourselves feeling something for them.

Why is that?

We love self–sabotaging ourselves and complain that there aren't any good men or women.

One hurt person can cause a domino effect for millions.

The many times that we've fallen in love and had hopes for it to never end or avoid negative opinions.

The truth is, life has never been fair, and when we learn instead of bullying ourselves, we win.

Why do we think that loving someone is so scary, but we're willing to give our bodies?

Why are we more comfortable being physically naked than to be explored mentally?

How different would this world be if we decided to love ourselves and others?

See, I can't accept the fact that people become angry and cold for no apparent reason.

Pour it out to me, and I'll show you why that only deserved to be one season.

I hope you can look at yourself in the mirror and see that you are so deserving of the smile that comes after the many tears.

"We grow through what we go through", so avoidance shouldn't be the reason we decide to shut our eyes and plug our ears.

If you want to be heard by them, prepare yourself to hear them.

We love telling stories from where we're coming from.

Ignoring the reality and the miscommunication that brought things there in the first place.

The most difficult thing to most is to look in the mirror and admit that we're the problem.

We're afraid of the truth, and if we fix ourselves, we'll lose that attention.

So, would you rather remain toxic and stagnant, or do you want to make the best of your life and become a caption?

About Him

She changed me.

I thought that I could play the game with her, but she showed me.

I didn't have to stay guarded this whole time.

She made me see that she wasn't going anywhere.

I wanted to cheat, but when I was presented with the opportunity, I had a blank stare.

It's like there was no one else out there who could step into what we share.

You've made a little boy want to become a man.

And I was willing to do what it took to be the one to hold your hand.

I thought that messing around with all these women would be something I'd do forever.

But you're the last person that I would ever want to hurt.

After getting my heart handed back to me unexpectedly, I gave up.

But you came in when I wasn't looking and brought back love.

I learned that what you do will turn right back to you.

And after breaking so many hearts, I had to get mine broken to appreciate you.

Lonely

Keep me company.
Hold my hand and kiss me softly.
Take my thoughts away.
I want to feel something today.

Tell me something I don't know.
Maybe then I'll stop taking it slow.
Nah, I'm lying. I'll still be guarded.
Because between us, it just started.

I only hit you up when I feel lonely.
And that's something you should see.
I won't be the one to tell you.
So, I hope you can read minds boo.

Xiomara Bastien

CHAPTER 5
HIDDEN EMOTIONS

This chapter is all about emotions and sometimes things we tend to avoid saying out loud.

Chapter 5 highlights the highs, the lows, the silent thoughts, daydreams, love, heartbreaks, and the many parts of ourselves we usually don't say aloud.

It's about how we take life on and sometimes what it does to us, and how we tend to handle things from our perspective.

In the world, we have doubts, fears, anger, depression, and overall, we tend to be our biggest critics.

For those of you reading this and who think you're alone, you are not. From all walks of life, most of us have something that we've been through that we didn't think that we would survive. Now, look at you, thriving and knowing that the past serves a lesson, not a way to shut down, but open yourself to other ways of living.

Cold

Ice.

I feel nothing, and I don't want to.

Lost in my own space, and I don't know who to turn to.

Or whether I should turn at all.

This was the kind of heartbreak that people warn you not to fall into.

One minute you're crying your eyes out; the next, you're numb.

I've pushed every single guy away who wanted to be without me because I'm done feeling dumb.

One day I'll figure out a way out of this feeling, but it's not looking like it'll be anytime soon.

Being alone is the only thing that doesn't make me feel like a fool.

I do my best to smile and be around people, but I truly don't care to.

Every guy after him. has seen a side that even he never was able to.

Distant, dry, cold and careless.

I mean, I'm sure one of them could bring me something endless.

I'm not ready to commit to anyone, but no one ever said anything about using your company.

I know I'm bitter, and somehow, even though I want to see it, I don't see myself being happy.

Space.

I wish I knew why I wanted space from you.

I try to find reasons why you're not the one for me.

Not sure if I trust you or if I'm willing to give myself completely.

I can be in love one day and annoyed the next, and I'll never know why.

Maybe from the other ones in the past, who's only objective was to make me cry.

I refused to be that girl a long time ago, so I can no longer be clingy.

I need space.

To go over and over in my head what I can do to sabotage something that made me feel free.

I want to find something wrong with you to use that one thing to end everything.

I need space.

I need to analyze everything you say because I know that we can't become something.

I need space.

To get other people's opinions and ignore what I feel because that's just who I am.

And I don't want these men thinking that they can come in and scam.

I need space.

I need to know that there's a part of you fighting for me when I'm not around.

I need to know that you won't leave me or be too proud.

I need space.

To be alone sometimes and overthink as I ask myself questions on whether you're the one or not.

I need to feel like I'm living in a fairytale and that my prince is better than that.

I need space.

To figure out if what I feel for you is actually real, and it's not just lust.

That's easy to pursue, so knowing your intentions is a must.

I need space.

Give me love when I'm near you but also know when I want to be solo.

Show me how you want to be loved, and I'll be different than most.

I just need space.

Space to explore my options and see if there's anything else out there that's better.

I know you could be good, but I have to make sure that you can be a partner.

I need space.

At least I think I do because even when I look at others, I always end up coming right back to you.

Forbidden

Love.

I mean, who can really describe it?

Can you tell me exactly the things that you're feeling?

Or is it a feeling that you like even when you can't describe it?

This is forbidden, you being from a lower class and me being considered high.

I knew people would have a lot to say about us, but that's something that I didn't mind.

When you finally revealed how you felt about me, for the first time, I didn't question it.

I felt safe, and I knew that with you, what we had was a perfect fit.

It's like you knew me more than I believed, especially when you noticed what I didn't say out loud.

But this is tricky, battling my head and my heart on what's really allowed.

Do I really care? Or am I more scared for you?

I am willing to keep this a secret as long as you stay true.

I told myself that I wouldn't make a mistake like this again.

Being in something that I know would create obstacles and bargain.

The way you made me feel has been present for such a long time, but now saying it to each other made things real.

I didn't want to hold back anymore because I wanted to go with how I feel.

When you kissed me the first time, it was weird; I didn't really know what it was.

But I knew I wanted to try again when your eyes were locked on me, pause.

I didn't regret doing it again because my whole body changed.

I couldn't get you out of my mind, I wanted to be around you every second; I hope that can be arranged.

I liked the way you looked into my eyes with so much hunger and desire.

I couldn't understand why we were both so willing to add fuel to the fire.

We knew that this was not supposed to happen between us.

But we couldn't help it; what we felt was stronger than anything else against us.

For now, though, this can remain a secret from everyone.

Until we figure out what this is and jump the gun.

I want you bad, and I can't control that for some reason.

So, I'll keep pursuing this with you until the end of our season.

I just knew

I knew you'd come back.

Those little girls weren't doing it for you, huh?

You thought I was going to stick around no matter what you did.

But baby, you're entirely wrong.

It's like you set the alarm every single time I moved on.

Because my phone would always ring when things for me were going strong.

Yes, I am the one who got away, and I know that for a fact.

You knew that I was a wife and not a girlfriend, which is why you didn't know how to act.

Why come back when I no longer want anything to do with you?

Why not be the right man for the woman you knew was right for you?

I guess you're stuck now.

Wondering what you'd do if I gave you another chance. I mean, really, how?

Walking away from you was the best decision that I've ever made.

And I will never regret what I did to put a smile on my own face.

I hope you were able to find everything that you thought you needed elsewhere.

Because the me that you don't know now has nothing for you and wholeheartedly doesn't care.

Torn

Two men.

So similar, yet so different.

I like them both for different reasons, and I can't make a decision.

Number 1, you came in unexpectedly, and a few conversations turned into something we both didn't know we needed.

We wanted the same things, and to me, you were too good to be true, but you showed me how I should be treated.

The chemistry was unmatched from the day we told each other how we felt.

I felt like you were the best hand I was ever dealt.

You were romantic, calm, smooth, sexy, and you wanted me.

Every word that came out of your mouth was like a sweet symphony.

I never knew I could feel something so fast, and yet I've known you for years.

Because we just decided to cross that line, it gave me chills.

You studied me, every inch of me just being, and you repeated things to me that you noticed.

None of them were physical, and that's when I knew I want you to be my focus.

The only part I'm concerned about is your constant worry of people knowing our business.

I mean, why not be a man and step up, letting everyone know who this is.

I'm not trying to pressure you; I just don't want to feel like your secret.

I don't need to be posted; I just want to feel like you're fighting for it.

I'm trying not to have any expectations, but you make it harder every time I see you.

Your passion and hunger for me could drive any woman crazy.

Number 2, I've wanted you for years.

At times I didn't even know if you ever noticed me.

You were my crush, and I wanted you to see me.

Times passed and I went on with my life, not knowing that you'd one day reach out to me.

The day you messaged me, I completely choked on my drink.

At first, I thought it was a mistake, but I had to pause, I didn't know what to think.

It turns out I was the one with who you wanted to start a conversation with.

It was instant, and it started before number 1 came in the picture to add a blur to it.

We had the same sense of humor, and I knew what to say to get you.

I guess it worked because I knew I would eventually run into you.

I wanted to see what you were about before making my last decision between you two.

I've never been in a situation where I would be this confused.

You both came into my life when I decided to love myself and explore things.

I knew I was going to stress because I wanted both of you for different reasons.

Number 1 should be a dead giveaway, but I want someone to fight to be with me.

And number 2, I don't want to go through life wondering how our interactions would be.

Number 1, you're who I need, and I feel so good when I'm near you.

The way you look at me makes me wonder what my life would be like with you.

But, there's fear.

I guess on both ends.

You want a love that's too secretive, and me being afraid to be loved the way you're ready to.

I don't want to self-sabotage because I will be the one to blame.

But wanting two people you truly feel could have the potential to be good for you is a shame.

I wish I could just choose, knowing I wouldn't want to be the second choice.

Number 1, I want you so bad it hurts me already.

But number 2, the possibilities for us are endless.

I'm torn; you'll find out who wins soon, I guess.

Silence

The lack of response alone tells me what I need to know.

Somehow, I still want you to open your mouth and let me know.

I hate standing around waiting for the answers to questions.

So, I'm going to have to find these things out on my own.

I want to move on as fast as my friends, but it's hard with the actions you've shown.

I want to know how to walk away as soon as I see a red flag instead of sticking around trying to fix someone.

And maybe that's what I should do, maybe to another man, I'll be his one.

Somehow what I thought I had with you was the opposite.

Because this wasn't love, this was one of the roadblocks that I had to hit.

I just don't know where to go from here.

I wish it was as easy to get over you like you got over me.

Bright Side

I keep hearing people talk about how much they want something real.

And yet, they're the same ones who can't hold up their part of the deal.

I, for one, love myself enough to know when efforts are either reciprocated or not

I base my decision off of how you act, and that determines who will be left to rot.

I never used to put myself first when it came to relationships.

Until the day that I realized that the one that mattered the most was the one with myself.

The more I dated, the more I added things that I didn't want in a life partner.

So the more lessons I learned benefitted me more than being a loner.

I always felt like I had guardian angels looking out for me.

Because the closer I would get to someone new, the quicker they would reveal their true selves to me.

I would just be myself each time, and they would either ruin the moment or disappear.

And I always counted those ghosts as undercover blessings.

I would rather know your intentions before I develop real feelings and eventually get physical.

I know that I deserve to be treated like a queen because my king wouldn't have a single worry.

I know he's out there somewhere making those mistakes and making it right with God.

So, I will continue to be the best woman for when you finally show up.

I love learning new things about myself because every failed situation taught me something.

And I'm grateful that I was in a space where I could turn those into what they've never seen.

My strength has grown, my confidence is unbreakable, and I am ready.

See, I have to see the world as the bright side.

Because what I have inside is nothing I should have to hide.

My tears will turn into endless oceans that will one day provide.

My experiences will help a little girl who may not be so sure of herself.

I want what I went through to find others and help.

I don't want the next woman to doubt herself because of what strangers say.

To the point that they feel like who they are isn't enough to stay.

Bright side, when you stop caring what people think, you become dangerous.

Because people try to find ways to get a reaction and panic when it's not a success.

Paranoid

I don't want you anywhere near me.

I always feel like you have the worse intentions when it comes to me.

You say all these beautiful words and even better actions, but what's the catch?

I can't trust that you're completely honest with me.

My past scars have shown me that sometimes it's hard to see.

So, it's better to be prepared for the worse.

I want to be able to not be surprised when this has reached its course.

I want you to leave me alone and stop trying to love me.

Because I don't know if I can trust something so healthy.

I wish you understood that about me because I don't know if I can offer you much.

I have this voice in my head telling me that you're just here to touch.

Paranoid.

I sometimes wonder if I can handle the love I say that I need.

Because half of me loves it when the other side is terrified of the speed.

Love Me More

I wish I could express how I felt to you.

We've been friends for years, and I can't see myself with anyone else but you.

You know me better than anyone else, and I know that you'd always be there.

You never left my side when I told you about my scare.

You held me and reminded me of how worthy I was and how much I deserved it all.

So, can you blame me for wanting to make that call?

I've had so many scenes in my head of how passionate things would be between us, but I don't want to ruin this.

I love you too much to be the reason you forget what love is.

I know I won't hurt you, but I also know how much

you've been hurt in the past.

I've seen you carry every scar, heartache, tear with pride and confidence.

So why would I want another man with what I know you'd fulfill? Science.

I can't dial your number without shaking.

So, you know what? I'll put my phone down and never express to you how I'm feeling.

Frozen.

Careless

I wish I didn't care.

I wish that I didn't get hurt every time I put myself out there.

I just wish I knew how to disconnect how I felt with how much I give.

I always expect to receive what I give out, but that's not the case.

So I need to understand that sometimes those people just needed to be loved at that moment.

I wish that I didn't care that my love and friendships weren't reciprocated.

Careless.

I take things personally, and I don't know how to turn that switch off.

I love others more than I love myself, and that's what

I'm scared of.

Putting myself first seems unnatural for me, and I just don't understand.

Being an empath is not what I thought it would be, and I sometimes can't stand it.

Maybe one day, it'll be my time to decide to put myself as the main priority.

But for now, let me fix someone else's crown as I ignore me.

No Filter

"I speak my mind even when I'm scared."

"I refuse to let people step all over me."

"I choose me and f**k how you feel."

"I play them faster than they could ever play me."

"Stop knocking on my heart door.

Because I won't be the one to let you in."

"I leave you before you even think about it."

"I don't give a f**k, and it's been working well for me."

Translation

I've been hurt far too many times to stay quiet.

People I trusted took advantage of me.

I've cared about people's opinions for too long.

I will not open my heart up for another one to break it.

My heart has been shattered too many times, and I had to repair it on my own.

I will walk away from you because I've gotten used to people walking away from me.

I've been isolating myself from everyone while I overthink in silence and drive myself crazy.

Different

Do people understand what it means to be different?

To be true to your unique abilities and share them with the world.

To see the world from your inner child's eyes instead of the skeptic adult.

It's ok to be your own person and not follow trends.

Bullies are only that when you let them put their insecurities onto you.

And when you give someone else power over you, you lose your individuality.

How they feel about you is not your problem, and that's how it should be.

When hate is spread faster than love, you can be who you are and change your mind immediately.

Different.

It's better to be you in all of your flaws and imperfections, than to be someone else.

Listening to negativity will have you be the same one trying to spread.

Different shouldn't be a fear.

Different is what makes the world see with different eyes and hear from different ears.

Petty

I see that you were able to step out on me multiple times.

Thinking that what you were slick and I wouldn't look at your infractions as crimes.

I've taken you back every single time, but now I'm going to have to draw this line.

Pack your s**t and get the hell out of my house!

What I bought, I kept.

So which car should I give you as a pity gift?

Oh, so you thought this would end on good terms?

Nah, you're gonna see the side that I've avoided for so long.

I mean, of course, I had to make sure you left with integrity, so I made sure your clothes were thrown out of the balcony folded.

Over ten years of me giving up everything to make sure you had your future molded.

No kids, the best of my years, and that's what you choose to fall back on.

I had enough proof of your infidelities to get everything in my name.

This time it won't be pretty, so I hope you're ready.

I was thinking maybe start by seducing your dad and becoming your stepmom.

I mean, he was interested in me first, and I kept my body fit so, maybe I should give him a call.

Let him take me on the trips that he promised me while we were married on a day in the fall.

I lost all senses when it comes to what you did to me, so it's time to be selfish.

I made sure that I gave you the least attractive car, especially when I knew how much you liked luxury.

My father's money was all you needed to stunt with other women while I took care of everything.

I stopped working, but now it's time to build back this empire on my own.

You can start from scratch; I'll have everything by the

time I'm done.

I was good to you.

I became the woman I swore I'd never become for you.

I wanted to make sure that you were able to shine all alone.

But that freedom went to your head, so you were always gone.

So, since I lost his number, can you tell your dad I'm free all weekend?

I tried to send a note, but the text wouldn't send.

Tell your new girl I said hi.

Click.

Not My Past

I am not who you knew five minutes ago, let alone five years ago.

Bringing up who I used to be or what I used to do doesn't help me grow.

You had to bring something up from back then because of the lack of access you have to me now.

I love it when people want to compare you to your childhood like it's where we reside.

I am right now, and I don't know what will happen next. I'm not on the side.

I'll stand in where I am and take in the moment as it goes.

I used to worry, scream, cry and hate what I saw in these clothes.

Now, I praise what I see because it represents beauty, especially with the scars.

I used to stay up nights wondering how things should be when I should've been embracing the stars.

I'm not my past.

You can keep bringing things up, and my favorite thing will be to just walk away.

I love the fact that I can set the boundaries I used to ignore and would stay.

My past formed me to now, but it doesn't define me.

Your judgments show exactly where I'd locate your insecurities.

I'll stay elevated, though.

Last I checked, I was busy, evolving and glowing.

Do the same, babe, and we can share the feeling.

I Don't Know

I say I want one thing, then I change my mind the next minute.

I say I want to be loved, but when it comes to me, I question it.

I'm starting to think I'm toxic.

Or maybe I haven't felt what I should when I have it in my hand.

I don't want to have any doubts, so I'll stay wherever I land.

I want a fun, joy-filled life.

But I don't take the necessary actions to get that freedom.

I wish I knew exactly what I had to do so that everyone can join.

But the stress that comes with success is what scares

me.

I don't know if I like being stagnant or if I'm letting my fear take control.

I think too much, and I wish I didn't because I know how far I could've been.

But I'll take things slow, and I'll speed up and eventually win.

All I know is that I know absolutely nothing.

So, I just end up thinking about all of the negative that I'm questioning.

Secret

I don't want to be anyone's 'on the low".

I want you but, I can't stay if there's no room to grow.

Your talk is sweet and all, but can you be mine long term? Or am I just another one of those girls for you to learn?

I can't believe much of what you say if your actions don't match.

It's easy to speak but, the reality is that this will most likely crash.

Yes. You're great at what you do, but I'm going to need more.

Sex is not what keeps me, so don't think that my brain is sore.

I won't overthink this time because I'll prolong what's inevitable. I get to see reality for what it is instead of trying to change it, not acceptable.

I'm Here

I want to remind you that I'm still standing.

No matter how many times you attacked my whole being.

Trying to be strong when it seems like the world hates you is a challenge.

But if I keep that mindset, there will be no change.

I want to tell you that I'm still here.

Fighting for the life that you tried to get me to end, but now it's clear.

You gave love the only way you knew how and I guess I was that love punching bag.

Many times, I convinced myself that I deserved to be tagged.

I want to remind you that I never left or listened to the negativity.

I made sure that whatever move I made was sneaky.

Off-grid, working on the pieces you tried so hard to break.

I get to remind them that they're whole again, and there's a part that you didn't take.

It's sad when your own seems to attack you the most.

But it's worse when you show them that in your head, they're the host.

Scarred

People love telling lies.

That's why I refuse to trust.

Secrets ruin lives.

And I know that describes us.

I want to give second chances, but I can't.

Because the constant flashbacks sting.

If I can't trust family, then why trust you?

They'd sell me in a heartbeat, so why wouldn't you?

I can't let myself go.

I can't let my guard down.

Because based on my track record, I don't deserve to be happy.

Instead of getting what I deserve, I get aroused by toxicity.

Because that's the love that I grew up to know.

I convinced myself that was the way to go.

I can't offer you anything but pain.

Because growing up, that's all I could claim.

Deserving

I choose to put myself first.

Get away when I need to breathe.

Stay quiet when I don't need to speak.

Laugh whenever I get the chance.

Maybe one day start a new romance.

Because I deserve it.

I accepted too much abuse to believe I deserved it.

I let others brainwash me when I knew better.

So now, it's my turn to feel good.

My turn to leave when I want and travel.

My turn to smile for no reason and reach a new level.

I deserve it.

I deserve to be taken out on dates.

To be hugged when I feel weak.

To be kissed when I talk too much.

I deserve it.

I deserve to reach my full potential.

To make my mark.

To always feel special.

I deserve it.

I spent too many years convincing myself that I didn't.

So many years believing all the words they say and...

So many more years convincing myself that they were right.

This time, I won't hold back.

I won't be scared to get what I want.

I won't let others dictate the way I think.

And I definitely won't take another undeserving man.

I deserve more.

I deserve to be respected.

To be cherished and appreciated.

I deserve to love hard without the fear of heartbreak.

I deserve more.

I deserve to work hard for my dreams and make them happen.

To not be afraid to fail because it happens.

To prove to myself that I can do it all.

I deserve it.

I am who I say I am.

So today, I'm deserving.

Xiomara Bastien

CHAPTER 6
FINISH STRONG

Chapter 6 is for every person who has felt any of the emotions in these poems.

It's a conversation that people avoid having with themselves and others.

Chapter 6 is to show every single person that, even with the world's ways of trying to bring you down, you will not let that change who you are.

It's a message for every person who has ever felt like they don't have a purpose or what it takes.

Just the simple reminder that no matter what obstacles come your way, you have the power to transform all that's considered bad into a blessing.

Dear Friend

I know that you've been hurt before.

You've hidden sides of yourself due to fear of judgment.

At times, I know that it seems like the world is against you.

Like you don't have anyone who will be a stand for you.

I know that sometimes it seems like there's no way out.

But all of these are getting you ready for so many more things to come.

Every sting has a purpose.

Every word that tried to hit you has growth in it.

Every heartbreak has a lesson for a bigger blessing.

You will make it out alive.

Any thought that crosses your mind trying to convince you that you're not enough is a lie.

Any bully (including yourself) trying to convince you that the world would be better off is a liar.

And when I say you're a bully to yourself, I mean that you allow how others see you to dictate how you see yourself.

When you were growing up, you saw the world through different lenses.

You saw possibilities as endless, and you believed in your dreams.

So, what changed?

Bullies?

Emotions?

Lies?

Deceit?

Unworthiness?

Tell me.

When did your light stop shining, and you let others tell you who you are?

How did it feel when you heard something negative and untrue about yourself?

And why did it affect you so deeply when you knew they weren't factual?

I would like to know.

I'm asking because that used to be my life.

The constant crying over men who didn't value me.

The suicidal thoughts that made me want to just quit.

The hating myself and my body because others with the same hate tried to take my joy away.

The anger, the grudges and frustration that I let convince me that life would always be that way.

Talk to me.

Tell me where it all started.

I want to understand the scars, the ugly, the hurt and help you heal.

I don't want you to ever feel like life is not worth living.

Or that you don't deserve happiness.

That toxicity is normal, and that something has to be wrong if it's too good to be true.

You are more than you give yourself credit for.

I want you to know that whoever didn't look your way twice is doing you a favor.

That the guy/girl you want and doesn't want you doesn't deserve you.

That even though life isn't always the way you'd like it to be, it's still beautiful.

I am here to listen, and I am here to remind you that you're not alone.

We've all been through traumatic experiences that helped shape who we are today.

But what we fail to realize is that we hold on to what we call negative much more than positive.

It's sad to see amazing people not see what they bring to the rest of the world.

Yes, I'm talking to you.

I know what you can create.

I know that you're the only you in the world.

That no one else can do what you can, the way that you do.

Take each moment, whether you consider it good or

bad.

And create something out of it.

Make those who doubted you regret the day that they tried to destroy you.

Or make them hate on you even more by not reacting to their comments or actions.

You are the only you.

No one will have the impact that you do.

Because either way, whether you're doing well or not, they will always find a reason to bad mouth you.

So, what do you choose?

Will you let insecure people bring you down?

Or will you make the decision to rise above it?

No one said that it would be easy.

But one thing is certain.

Whatever you decide to do for yourself.

Make sure you're not doing it for anyone else's approval.

Because it's always funny when we value others'

opinions more than our own.

And those same people never ask us for our opinions on how they should live their own lives.

Remember that all we have is right now, and in one minute, it'll be the past.

Any opportunity you get to live, laugh, go on an adventure or just simply be alone, go for it.

Don't let anyone belittle who you are or what you do.

It's time to take your life into your own hands and seek guidance from God and those who walked a similar path before you did.

Because those who have things going for themselves don't have the time to talk about you.

Whoever you are reading this, I want you to know that I love you.

All your obstacles, smiles, tears and thoughts were all present for a purpose.

And you have the power to make something amazing out of every experience.

Thank you for being a beautiful human.

You are loved.

King/Queen

Never let anyone try to convince you to put your crown down.

Walk with pride, knowing that unlike many others, you won't drown.

You won't follow what others do. You're in your own lane.

And there's beauty in knowing that all paths aren't the same.

No matter what or who tries to trigger you into quitting, walk away.

Everything you desire is in front of you, just don't allow yourself to be led astray.

I know distractions feel good at the moment, but what about what comes after?

Are you willing to have a temporary pleasure instead of a permanent closer?

If that went over your head, let me explain.

You know what you want, but you allow others you like to change that.

Sometimes you ignore red flags and go for it anyway, and for what?

Lessons are usually learned that way but how many times?

Will you learn from them or make an excuse as to why you're tolerating it again.

King/Queen, you represent gold. You have so much love and soul.

I challenge you to stop caring what others think and go for what you know is right for you.

Ignore those who want to discourage you when they were never supposed to be part of your story.

When you are elevating, many will not make those steps.

So, when you start losing "friends", don't be surprised and start counting your reps.

People who no longer serve you will start to show themselves and drop like flies.

And it's your job to thrive and still follow that dream

and walk in your purpose.

Many will not understand your passion, but they're not supposed to.

Our paths are different, and each experience molds us, so how are others supposed to understand?

No one is you, and that's the power that you hold in your hands.

Many may do the same thing, but they will never do it the way that you do.

Be who you are and also ask yourself if you would want to be with someone like you.

And if the answer is no, there's a lot of self-love that gets to come from you to you.

I dare you to love yourself and speak to you how you would speak to those you love.

And watch how things change, how much joy comes in and how it's easy to surrender.

Working hard on a dream and believing in it, sometimes alone, is where the magic lies.

So the next time someone wants to discourage you, say nothing, and let that success hypnotize.

Never let your crown fall King/Queen.

ABOUT THE AUTHOR

Xiomara Bastien has been a fan of the arts her entire life, especially writing and dancing. She was exposed to the art world through her father, who always made sure that she had the opportunity to see the world differently. Xiomara was raised in Port-au-Prince, Haiti, and she continues to travel there to see her family. Xiomara received her Bachelor's degree in Psychology in 2014 from the University of Toledo, Ohio. She has a passion for helping others, and writing happens to be one way she relates to the world. Xiomara is currently in graduate school for her MBA in International Business and plans to have her own business overseas. Xiomara's an influencer, whose ultimate goal is to become a speaker, coach and Bestselling author, while helping others with self-love and reminding every person of their worth.

Xiomara Bastien

WE HAVE MANY SIDES, WHAT'S YOURS?

A SERIES OF POEMS THAT CONNECTS MILLENNIALS IN A WORLD OF CHAOS.

XIOMARA. B

Grab my free poem and allow it to empower and encourage you to keep going and never give up. You have a purpose and your voice matters. Don't give up. People need you and you are on this earth for a reason.

Visit My Website
xiojenbas.wixsite.com/my-site-2